The Witness

Joanna Nadin ■ Jonathan Edwards

OXFORD
UNIVERSITY PRESS

Saturday

Something BAD has happened. The sort of BAD that Dad says is spelled with a capital B. It is all because I didn't go to football practice. Mainly because I get picked last every week and Hedgehog Hogan kicks me every time I miss a ball (which is a lot).

I have begged Dad about a million times not to make me go. He says it is good for me or I will be a couch potato. He doesn't want me to be like Harry down the road, who hardly ever plays out. Anyway, instead I went to `The Hut´, which is the park keeper´s hut on the playing field.

The lock is broken at the side, so you can get in and hide in there. Sometimes I go there after school. Mostly I have to go home or Dad says he will worry and call out the cavalry, whoever they are. Anyway, I was in The Hut, reading *The Adventures of Hans Hero*. I heard a noise outside.

I looked out of the slats on the window and it was the Parry twins. They are called Gary and Barry, which is funny when you think about it. They weren't actually being funny. They were doing something BAD to Sean Hawkes who is in our class. He had blood on his nose.

The Parry twins took something out of Sean's bag, which was a new bag with a picture of Hans Hero on it. Then I knew what they were doing. They were doing BULLYING – which Miss Hicks told us about last year. She said if we were bullied, we had to tell our mums or dads or tell her. And that there was nothing shameful about being bullied.

The ones who should be ashamed are the BULLIES.

The Parrys never look ashamed. Not even when they took Andy Thomas's crisps every day for a month. Or when they made Steven Warren drink blue ink, which made him sick – which was blue as well. So I thought about whether I should tell Dad. If I do, he will go mad because then he will know I was in `The Hut', which is `out of bounds'. He'll also know that I was not at football. Maybe Sean will tell his mum anyway. Then it will be OK. I must have made a noise because Gary turned round and saw me looking out of the window.

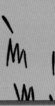

The BAD thing has got worse. Gary and Barry Parry came round to our house this afternoon. I was playing outside on the mini trampoline. Dad came out and said, "Your friends are here, Edward. They are in the living room." I went in because I thought it might be Steven Warren and his brother. But it wasn't.

It was the Parrys and they were sitting on the green sofa. They both had on exactly the same shoes and tracksuits. Dad said, "Would you boys like some lemonade?" They said, "yes" but I said, "no". Then, when Dad went to get it from the kitchen, Gary said, "Have you told anyone about yesterday?"

I know it was Gary because his head is bigger and he also has a gold G on a necklace. I said, "No". He said, "Well, don't or it'll be you next, Eddie Quick." I said that I wouldn't tell anyone. Which I know is bad because Miss Hicks said you must always tell someone, but I don't want to get beaten up by Gary or Barry.

Then Barry said, "Anyway, that Sean Hawkes is a baby. He cried even before I did his nose." And I said, "Yeah." Then Gary said that Sean should be called Boo-hoo Sean instead, and they both started laughing like hyenas.

Then Barry said to me that Quick is a stupid name. He said that I should be called Eddie Slow because I am not very quick at all – and then they laughed some more. I laughed too. Because it is a bit funny even though it is not very nice. Barry said, "You're all right, Slow Eddie." And I said, "Thanks."

Then Dad came in with the lemonade and little cakes with jam in the middle and they ate four each. I am only ever allowed two at once. I didn't tell them that or they might stop thinking I am all right and beat me up anyway. Then they got bored because my computer doesn't have good games on it. Gary said, "See you in school, Slow Eddie." And I said, "Yeah."

Then they went home. The Parrys are 'good as gold' when they're at home. Harry's Uncle Dave lives next door to the Parrys, and he told us.

During dinner, which was pizza, Dad said, "Your friends seem nice, Edward", and I said, "Yeah." But they are not nice really.

Sean Hawkes has a big scratch on his arm just under his shirt sleeve. He sat next to me at lunch. Harry normally sits there except he is off with a dodgy tummy since he came back from his holiday. Sean said, "You have to tell someone what you saw. Then there will be two of us."

I could see the Parrys two tables away and Gary did the sign which means `I'm watching you'. He got it from a film. So I said, "What are you talking about, Hawkesy?" Sean said, "I know you were there at The Hut, Eddie." But I could still see Gary watching me, so I said that I needed the toilet.

I didn't eat my pudding even though it was a chocolate chewy bar. I just got up and went to the toilet. Gary gave me the thumbs up sign. I stayed in there for eleven minutes until lunch was over. I didn't even come out when Miss Hicks knocked on the door and said, "Is everything all right in there, Edward Quick?"

I said, "Yes, thank you." She said, "Well, if you've got a tummy upset, you'd better go home. We don't want an epidemic." Whatever that is. I said I didn't. Even though I really did want to go home.

Next was maths, which is OK because the Parrys go to a different class.

At afternoon break it was raining and so we had to stay in the classroom. I had to go into the book corner and Barry said, "Did you say anything, Slow Eddie?" I said, "No way!" So Gary said, "Nice one." Then he said to meet them at the gate after school. "We've got something for you."

After school I tried to be really quick. I put my jacket on even before the bell went because I said I was cold. Miss Hicks said I didn't look cold, I looked sweaty. Then Mr Rose, who is our headteacher and is called Rambling Rose because he talks a lot, asked me to help him carry some books to the library. Of course I had to because otherwise Rambling Rose would make me stay after school.

So when I got to the gate, the Parrys were already there. Gary said, "Here you go." It was a box with a game in and it was the racing game they stole off Sean at `The Hut`. I said, "No thanks," but Barry said, "Take it because your computer's useless at the moment." I remembered Sean's scratched arm and I thought I didn't want one so I took it and put it in my bag.

Dad clears my bag out when I get home because sometimes I leave apple cores in it. Once one rotted until it was black. So when I got home, I ran upstairs and put the game right under my bed where it is all dusty. Dad knocked on the door and said, "Are you all right, Edward? Is something wrong?" I said, "No, I am fine."

Then I came out and gave him my bag to clear out and we went downstairs and watched our quiz show. All the time I could feel the game under my bed like it was shouting out and I kept thinking Dad would hear it. I felt sick and I could only eat one chocolate finger. Normally I can eat at least eight.

The Parrys are doing more BULLYING. They are making Sean pay them his £1.50 lunch money every day. They are going to split it three ways and I get 50p. I have to be the lookout and make sure Rambling Rose isn't coming. I said they could keep it and split it 75p each. Barry said, "No way! You're one of us now, Slow Eddie."

So they got Sean in the toilets and made him hand over the money. I stayed at the door and looked out to make sure no teachers were coming. When Steven Warren asked to come in, I said, "No". He had to go to the baby toilets, which are really low down and your knees stick up in the air.

Taking Sean's lunch money was REALLY BAD because what I forgot to say is that Sean has Type 1 diabetes.

Sean cried and said that if he didn't eat something his blood sugar would get low and he would feel funny and become unwell. Which is true. It happened once in PE. Sean went pale and shaky and Miss Butterworth, the school secretary, had to give him a sugary drink and a biscuit. We didn't think it was fair that Sean was having a biscuit in PE, but we knew that he had to have it. Like medicine.

Gary told Sean to tell Miss Hicks he'd lost his money. So he did. And she made sure he had some lunch.

Our next lesson was citizenship and Miss Hicks showed us a film about a girl who is BULLIED by two bigger girls who aren't real. They are acting. Then afterwards she asked us what we thought and whether the girl should have talked to someone. Then she looked straight at me, so I think she knows I am helping to do BULLYING.

Gary flicked an elastic band at my head. It hit Stacey instead and she cried. Gary got sent to Rambling Rose and we did collages instead after that. I could feel the 50p in my pocket, all loud and hot and bright like the computer game.

I thought someone would see it, so before lunch I put it in Miss Hicks' collection box for poor children. She said, "That is very kind, Edward. Are you sure you can spare it?" and I said, "They need it more than me." Then she said, "Well, you are a thoughtful boy." I felt even more sick.

Collection for
poor children
Thank you!

Sean brought sandwiches today, but Gary snatched them off of him. Sean cried and Barry said, "Shut up, Chicken Licken." Then they flushed the sandwiches down the toilet, which is just a waste. Then Gary said, "Come on, Eddie, I'm starving," because I was on lookout.

I kept looking at Sean, who had now curled up on the floor of the toilets, which smells and is a bit wet. So I said, "I need the toilet. I'll catch up." So Gary said, "All right." Barry said, "Don't be too long or you might catch something off Sean. Which isn't true. You can't *catch* diabetes.

I told Sean to get up, but he had gone pale and had started shivering. So I shook him gently. He still didn't get up, and I knew his blood sugar was low. And it was all my fault.

I shouted and shouted for Miss Hicks to come. But Rambling Rose opened the door and said, "What on earth is the matter?"

Then he saw Sean and said, "Go to the office and get Miss Butterworth to bring Sean's blood testing kit and his Hypo Box." I could hear a noise, and it was me crying. I was saying, "Sorry, Sean. Sorry, Sean." Rambling Rose said, "Get going, Edward!"

33

So I did and Miss Butterworth, who is trained in dealing with diabetes, came at once. She went to the toilets where the whole school was waiting to see what had happened. But Rambling Rose wouldn't let anyone in. Then Miss Hicks made us all go back to our classrooms.

She said that Sean's mum had taken him home as he wasn't feeling well. I felt sick too. I knew I had to stop joining in with the Parrys or I would feel sick every day.

So at last break I met them in the toilets, and I said I couldn't be their lookout anymore. Gary said, "You're just Chicken Licken like Sean." Barry said, "Say it. Say 'I'm a chicken.'" And he pushed me against the hand dryer. Then he said, "Say it, say it, say it." And the hand dryer was blowing and burning the back of my neck, so I said, "I'm a chicken." He let me go and they both laughed and did chicken noises. Then Gary said, "Watch your back, Slow Eddie." And he did the sign again that he was watching me. Now all the BAD stuff is worse than ever.

Thursday

I didn't go to school today. When I woke up I still felt sick because of the Parrys watching me all the time and planning BULLYING on me. Dad said, "Are you all right, son?" and I said, "No, I think I might be ill."

"Are you sure, because if you are not really sick you have to go because I can't afford to be off work." Even though I know he needs the money so he can buy our food and pay for football and everything, I said, "Yes, I am sure." I told him that I might have got what Harry has – a bad tummy for over a week.

Dad said, "Well, stay in bed and I'll get a bowl for you." I said, "OK." Then he came back with a big plastic bowl in case I really was sick. He put it under the bed next to the computer game. Later, after I had been in bed for a while, I got to lie on the sofa and watch TV all day.

I had noodle soup for lunch, and there was no one to be a lookout for or call me Chicken Licken. I thought of Sean again and whether he was still unwell. And whether the Parrys would keep stealing his sandwiches. Then I really did feel sick and went back to bed and didn't even have dinner.

Dad made me go to school. I said I was still sick, but he said I hadn't actually thrown up. He took my temperature under my armpit and said I was fine and that anyway he needed to get back to work. Then he took the bowl out from under the bed, but his fingers touched something else.

It was the computer game. He said, "Where did you get this, Edward?" and I felt sicker than ever. My face went hot. I couldn't think what to say fast like they do on the TV when they have to do a cover up, so I just cried instead. Dad said, "It's all right, son," and I said, "No, it isn't."

Dad said, "Just tell me what the matter is." I said, "It's from the Parrys. They stole it off Sean." Then he said, "Why have you got it?" I said, "I didn't go to football, Dad. I hid in 'The Hut' and I saw them beat up Sean, but I didn't tell and now they are my friends, except I don't like them." I said, "Now Sean is sick with his diabetes and the Parrys are going to beat me up instead." Dad said, "Calm down, son. Calm down." Amazingly I did. Because Dad stroked my hair really slowly like you stroke a cat and all the crying stopped.

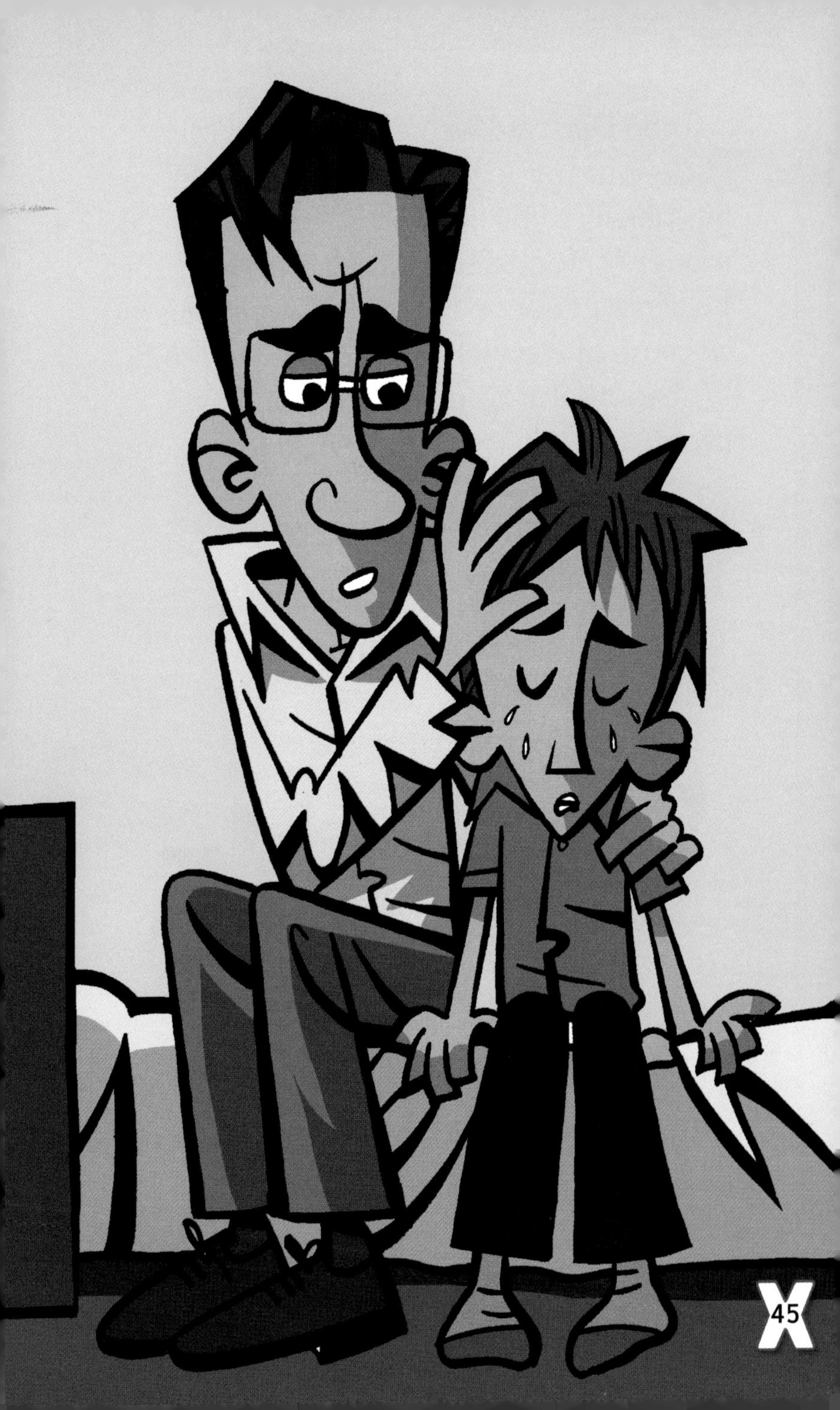

Then Dad said we needed to tell Miss Hicks what happened. I said, "I will tell her because you need to go to work to get money for food and football. I'm really sorry. I will never not go to football again. It is just because of Hedgehog Hogan." Dad said, "The football doesn't matter. But do you promise to tell Miss Hicks? And I said, "Yes."

And I did. I went to school and told her first thing. Then I gave her the game. Gary and Barry were watching me the whole time but they couldn't hear me. Miss Hicks said she was going to see Rambling Rose (except she said *Mr* Rose) and he came back. He asked for Gary and Barry to go with him please.

Gary did the 'I'm watching you sign', but I looked down at my Hans Hero book instead. Then Rambling Rose came back and asked for me to go with him. I felt sick and thought that the Parrys had said it was all my fault.

When I got to the office they weren't there. Sean was there instead. He was with his mum and looked much better. I said, "Sorry, Sean," again and he said, "It's OK." Rambling Rose said, "I am very disappointed in you, Edward, but I understand that you were also a VICTIM in this," and I said, "Yes."

He also said, "It was brave to tell Miss Hicks what you did and I have called your father to tell him you will not be punished this time." I said, "Thanks." Then he said that he takes BULLYING very seriously and that Gareth and Barrington (who are really Gary and Barry) will not be allowed to do it any more.

Then he said that me and Sean could go back to class and we did. At lunch Sean sat with me and Harry who is back from being sick. We shared Harry's crisps because he had two bags – Salt and Vinegar and Cheese and Onion, which I like best. I didn't feel sick at all until I remembered I had football in the morning.

Saturday

The Parrys are definitely being punished. Rambling Rose called Sean's mum last night and said he'd had a meeting with their parents. Gary and Barry have to stay after school every day for counselling until they learn how to behave properly. Their mum has to walk them to school and pick them up at the gate and they can't play in the playground at break or lunch times.

Sean told me when he came round this morning. I didn't go to football. Dad said if I hated it that much there was no point him forking out every week for it. It was OK as long as I go swimming instead and don't turn into a couch potato. So I am going to go to the pool tomorrow with Sean. When we have finished building a rocket out of the lemonade bottle and a yoghurt pot.

Harry is coming too because when he jumps off the diving board the whole pool jumps out. It is excellent. And even if the Parrys are going swimming too it doesn't matter because there are three of us. Plus they are scared of Harry because of his Uncle Dave who lives next door to them and has a huge dog.

Dad said, "I hope you have learned a lesson, son," and I said, "I have." Then it was time for Sean's afternoon snack. Dad got us chocolate fingers and we ate three each. Then Harry came round and ate nineteen chocolate fingers, which is a new record and we are going to write to television to tell them.